VINEYARD FOLK

VINEYARD FOLK

*creative people and places
of martha's vineyard*

TAMARA WEISS AND AMANDA BENCHLEY

PHOTOGRAPHS BY ELIZABETH CECIL

ABRAMS, NEW YORK

Editor: Rebecca Kaplan
Designer: Stephanie Huntwork
Design Manager: Darilyn Carnes
Managing Editor: Lisa Silverman
Production Manager: Larry Pekarek

Library of Congress Control Number: 2022947982

ISBN: 978-1-4197-6381-6
eISBN: 979-8-88707-063-6

ABRAMS The Art of Books
195 Broadway, New York, NY 10007
abramsbooks.com

CONTENTS

foreword by Carly Simon 8
introduction 12

MICAH THANHAUSER 16
JULI VANDERHOOP 24
ROSE STYRON 32
KRISHANA COLLINS 40
NETTIE KENT AND COLIN RUEL 50
MARK CHUNG AND ERIC COLES 58
MARGOT DATZ 68
GOGO FERGUSON AND DAVE SAYRE 76
JOHN AND LARA FORTÉ 86
KATE TAYLOR 94
HEATHER GOFF AND BILL O'CALLAGHAN 104
FLAVIA GAETA 112
BEN TAYLOR 118
ALLEN AND LYNNE WHITING 126
JESSICA B. HARRIS 136
AMY BRENNEMAN AND BRAD SILBERLING 144
MICHAEL JOHNSON 156
BROOKE ADAMS 164
VALERIE FRANCIS 174
LEXIE ROTH AND EVA FABER 178
JULIE TAYMOR AND ELLIOT GOLDENTHAL 188
TIFFANY VANDERHOOP 196
KARA TAYLOR 204
ZACH PINERIO 212

Tune In/Tune Out 220
Ocean of Thanks 270

As long as this island sits in the sea, chances are artists will always be called to discover its secrets. Why the Vineyard? Follow some of these artists through the pages of this book and decide for yourself. After all . . . we have no secrets.

When I first came to the Vineyard as a baby, the island was my sandbox for play. As I grew older, sand became song and song became play. So many songs written and played over the years . . . so many grains of sand through so many fingers of so many storied figures.

I am very fortunate always to have been a character in this creative story. I'm honored to call many of the artists and personalities whose tales are told here friends and family. As we grow up and our creativity matures, hopefully we'll still have the seeds of those shining days in the sandbox that lured us out to the west of Lambert's Cove.

To the best of my memory, here is a timeline of my early musical adventures on the Vineyard:

Nine and a half months old: Had chicken pox (wrote no songs).

Thirteen months old: "Itsy Bitsy Spider," my first "tick."

Three years old: "The Wabash Cannonball," an old folk song sung at the next-door neighbor's house on Flanders Lane in Menemsha. Raw shrimp, yuck.

Four years old: Sang "Itsy Bitsy Spider," this time at the Agricultural Fair in West Tisbury. (Wondered if the song had been written by a real spider, or just another human who happened to have been washed down a spout or two?)

Eleven years old: Sister Lucy sets a Eugene Field poem, "Wynkin, Blynkin, and Nod," to music. (We sang it all the time, and we always will.)

Twelve years old: Davey and Jessie (my idols) make me want to write songs. "Doctor Freud" and "Roll On, Columbia, Roll On."

Thirteen years old: Sang "Wild Mountain Thyme" at Max Eastman's house in Gay Head (which is now called Aquinnah).

Fifteen years old: "Hava Nagila" and the Fireside Book of Folk Songs on Menemsha Inn Road. (Baba ganoush and do-si-do. Two for the price of one.)

Sixteen years old: Sang "Blue Skies" with sisters Lucy and Joey in a perfect three-part harmony on Menemsha Inn Road. (This is getting serious.)

Seventeen years old: Started writing songs. The first one was "Hold Back the Branches," based on a Spanish poem. (Written in my bedroom on a flamenco guitar.)

Nineteen years old: Lucy and I performed at the Moon-Cusser Coffee House as "The Simon Sisters" for the first time. (Drove home drunk with brand-new licenses. Oy vey.)

Twenty-one years old: One of the first concerts performed with Livingston Taylor at the Martha's Midsummer Night's Moon Festival. Sung "In My Reply" (at my brother Peter Simon's rented house in Vineyard Haven).

Twenty-four years old: Wrote "Alone" and "One More Time" on Squibnocket Beach, and "Look Me in the Eyes" in Vineyard Haven.

From that point on, many of my artistic endeavors have been like the haze of inspiration. At once so misty and all of a sudden so clear.

For as far back as I can recall, the Vineyard seems to have been made to tolerate artists like me. It's the perfect haven, a sacred vessel for all the other sacred vessels. I've written more than a hundred songs here and feel that a hundred more are waiting, if only I can just get down to the sea.

—CARLY SIMON
HIDDEN STAR HILL
MARTHA'S VINEYARD
2022

The creative energy on Martha's Vineyard runs like a bolt of lightning from one end of the island to the other.

It begins with the Aquinnah Wampanoag people of Noepe (Martha's Vineyard), who, for more than ten thousand years, have imbued the island with their traditions, artistry, and culture, and whose descendants continue to keep their traditions alive. Driving down-island through Chilmark, following the lichen-covered stone walls, one can imagine farmers' hands, hundreds of years ago, placing together rocks by weight with no mortar, building walls that lasted centuries. Or picture the great painter Thomas Hart Benton, as he captured the pastoral scenes and people for more than fifty years, beginning in 1920. And all the way down-island, Harlem Renaissance writer Dorothy West made Oak Bluffs her home and the setting of her novel *The Wedding*. The Island's beauty and mystery endure as a magnet for artists.

I have been coming to the Vineyard my entire life, eventually moving here full-time twenty-seven years ago with my then husband and twin toddlers. We found an old farmhouse in need of repair, opened a store called Midnight Farm with my longtime friend Carly Simon, and watched as our sons grew from "island boys" to men.

Midnight Farm was more than a store. Customers and friends alike joined together for evenings of poetry, author readings, and concerts, or to peruse a designer's latest creations. Countless wonderful people walked through our doors, and a welcoming, creative, and diverse community was formed. Its exuberance blossomed into a long tradition of weekly potlucks at our home—sitting around the backyard firepit, guitars passed from one to another, songs flowing like wine late into the night.

I have now lived here long enough to appreciate the history of those who chose to make Martha's Vineyard their creative home. So when my friend Amanda Benchley planted a seed for a book about artists living on Martha's Vineyard, I was quick to say yes. Celebrating the talents of artists and their individual stories of inspiration drawn from the island felt timely—and necessary—as economic changes threaten the artistic community I love.

While many of those featured in the pages of this book are more-than-comfortably settled, others have spent years doing the "Vineyard Shuffle," moving from one place to another, usually dictated by the summer season. Buying a home here is a stretch for any member of our workforce, much less an artist or a young family beginning to find their way.

Many are determined to make it work, even if it means not quite knowing where they will be living next year. There is something about this island. Like the gravitational pull of a full harvest moon on the waves at Squibnocket, the bond between artist and island is strong. Still, sadly, others have been forced to leave, carried out by the economic tide.

We spoke to potters, painters, farmers, poets, musicians, curators; just some of the hundreds of Vineyard Folk who are part of the artistic community and who have wonderful stories to tell. Photographer Elizabeth Cecil has captured them with her evocative images at their homes and in their workspaces, documenting them at this pivotal time.

To the island artists who share Martha's Vineyard as their muse, may you flourish and continue to contribute to the rich, beautiful history of this place we call home. And to the future generations of artists, we are counting on you to keep shining, like the red and white beam from the Gay Head Lighthouse, or that bolt of lightning from one end of the island to the other.

—TAMARA WEISS

There's something about living on a semi-remote island, where everything from bread to plumbing parts comes in on a boat, that requires an adventurous spirit and the wearing of many different hats. So it's not really a surprise that so many people in the pages of this book—and on Martha's Vineyard itself—are "multi-hyphenates." Kate Taylor is a singer-songwriter-jewelry designer-artist. Margot Datz is a painter-illustrator-muralist. We had to shorten John Forté's self-description from "singer-songwriter, composer and filmmaker, and activist" for lack of space, not because he isn't all those things.

But the more remote, the more magical: the place and the people. I started spending time on the Vineyard in the summer of 2018, with the great good fortune of Tamara as my fairy godmother. As she famously does, she graciously and lovingly folded me into her vast, varied circle right away. What I immediately noticed was the remarkable informality of Vineyard gatherings: Dinners were potluck, jeans and flip-flops worn, and there was always a refreshing mix of ages, backgrounds, and income levels. But what was equally obvious was how talented everyone was. It was perfectly normal to sit next to someone wearing jewelry she had designed herself or for guests to pick up guitars and start singing around the fire after dinner.

Enough of these evenings led to the question that then led to the idea for this book: Why are so many creative people drawn to this New England island, seven miles off the coast of Cape Cod?

So together, Tamara and I set out to uncover why. The allure of the island's majestic beauty and legendary beaches of course popped up as constant inspiration. There's also a long tradition of art and craft of all kinds on the island, partially due to the abundance of natural materials: clay in the soil that can be made into pottery, the very alive bodies of water that beg to be painted, a bounty of offerings from the sea and the land to be turned into delicious meals, countless vistas to stare out into and dream of stories.

But, in my opinion at the end of this journey, the community—these Vineyard folk and their unique, creative synergy—is the key. There is so much mutual support and cross-pollination. Brooke Adams credits the influence of Allen Whiting—and *his* mentor/idol Stan Murphy—on her painting; Amy Brenneman and Brad Silberling display work by Colin Ruel and Kara Taylor on their walls and have a fire pit built by Ben Taylor. Carly Simon has commissioned Margot Datz to paint murals on nearly every door and wall of her house. The Ruel and the Forté kids go to school together. So much overlap and wonderful collaboration.

And that's the way it has always been, turns out. For me, the process of writing this book was a hands-on, nose-deep education on this special island and its people. And as a result, Tamara and I have created a kaleidoscopic snapshot of creativity from this very particular moment of time while also trying to remember and honor the history of the island creators of the past. We and the Vineyard Folk welcome you to dive into these stories.

—AMANDA BENCHLEY

MICAH THANHAUSER

potter

Micah Thanhauser will immediately jump off his pottery wheel and into his pickup truck anytime a friend spots a newly uncovered jackpot of clay at a nearby construction site. He will then bring the treasured raw material back to his combination gallery and studio, tucked away on Merry Farm Road in West Tisbury.

It's this natural island clay, combined with glazes made from the burned ash of trees in Micah's yard, that creates the unprocessed and patina feel of his tableware and pottery that are so specific to Martha's Vineyard. He learned this practice while studying in Japan, where attention to local material is integral in the formation of pottery.

"We do have every material that a potter would need," he says, "which isn't true of most places." Clay found in Chilmark is filled with rocks and sticks, but according to Micah, "you can pick it right out of the earth and make a pot of it, no problem," which you can't do with the sandier clay that is found near the remains of the island's famous nineteenth-century brickyard. "The island has an interesting geology," he says. "Some areas are sand, some are a mix of sand and clay, and some are just all clay."

Raised down the road from his current studio, Micah returned to the island following college and a three-year apprenticeship in the pottery mecca of Asheville, North Carolina. Moving back was always in the cards though. "I think the ocean, the feeling of history, and the feeling of belonging were the draw," he says.

"The memories and feelings of being a kid here resonate."

The island's distinct landscape, especially the majestic red clay cliffs of Aquinnah, holy ground for the Wampanoag tribe, also inspires his work. "I go to Aquinnah all the time and vibe out. That clay is ancient, hundreds of millions of years old," he says. When he's not there, Micah and his young family—wife Emily, two-year-old Asa, and baby Mae—head to Lambert's Cove and Cedar Tree Neck, or walk around the trails in the woods. They bought the building from island boat builder Frank Rapoza, who insisted on selling only to a fellow artist, and now live above the studio in an apartment that still bears Frankie's touch: The tiny, well-built kitchen actually feels like the galley of a boat.

Micah currently works with a gas-fired kiln, but his eyes light up when talking about his plans to build a large wood-burning kiln to share with the entire island pottery community. Not only is there a tradition in pottery of communal firing, but he also wants to experiment with the different, more spontaneous effects that firing with wood brings to the craft. And, naturally, he plans to burn old dock pilings, saturated with salt, in the kiln to be sure his works are island-made through and through.

"I am trying to learn as much as I can about the history of the island and the geology," he says.

A sampling of Micah's finished work on display. "I'm making things that feel like they can be at home in nature."

and washing

ighting fixtur

arge hollow form

All sizes & styles o

VASE

A wood-burning stove keeps
Micah's studio warm.

JULI VANDERHOOP

tribal/community activist, business owner

Juli Vanderhoop learned to bake by watching her stepfather, Luther Madison, the medicine man of the Wampanoag tribe of Gay Head (Aquinnah), prepare pies for the Aquinnah Shop, her mother's restaurant at the head of the Aquinnah cliffs. Working at the restaurant was a rite of passage for local kids, and her mother, Anne Vanderhoop, was at the center of the action, chatting with every customer and friend who stopped by.

Now a couple of miles down State Road, Juli is carrying on the traditions of warm hospitality and Luther's homemade pies at the Orange Peel Bakery, built on historic land her mother gave her. "Community is so important," says Juli, who stops to answer questions from first-time bakery visitors as a friendly rooster totters around her feet.

On the bakery's popular pizza nights, Juli, as her mother did, mingles with the hungry crowd, encouraging everyone to share pizza toppings and become friends while their pizzas bake in the oversized, whale-shaped oven that Juli built with local stones. Some nights, DJ-led, interactive ecstatic dances or story-driven music and dance performances curated by the Yard take place behind the bakery, on a stage in the woods where diners are often invited to jump in.

The bakery came from Juli's desire to connect people to each other and to the land that has been in her family for generations. The Wampanoag tribe settled the "land surrounded by water," formerly known as Gay Head, on the island's narrow far-western region centuries ago. When she wasn't hanging out at the Aquinnah

Shop, Juli's childhood was spent trailing after six older brothers as they wandered the area's heaths and beaches. In summer they would spend all day outside, foraging for blueberries, drinking out of the Black Brook stream, and dragging home freshly caught fish as big as they were.

"We are people who have been here a very long time, and growing up here, running around and being as wild as the elements themselves, risking your life whether you were in the water or near the water, shaped you and tested your will to really survive," she says. "My mom always said that people from Gay Head were always known as very strong."

Juli also serves as a select person on the Aquinnah town council, ensuring that the same vibe and community she's creating at the bakery are preserved in the town as well. With the council, she is currently working to create an open space in the center of town—filled with communal gardens, walking trails for elders, and a basketball court—that will be a gathering place for everyone. "I created a business that can help the community; it's not about the bottom line," she says. "This is such a beautiful place, we don't want to see chain stores here."

Back at the bakery, a team of local teenage boys are learning to braid challah, one of the many breads Juli has for sale. "I tell them that theirs will never look like mine because I have been doing this for sixteen years," she says. "But when they eat it, it's going to be OK. We don't want to be cookie cutter; we are looking for country wild."

Juli imported the oven from France and then hand-built the surround with local stones. "We wanted it to look like it's been here for a hundred years," she said.

Juli monitoring the Orange Peel's
famous baguettes and pies.

The Urban Bush Women dance troupe and Juli bring community together on Pizza Night.

ROSE STYRON

poet, human rights activist

❚ understand why writers are here," says ninety-four-year-old poet, journalist, and human rights activist Rose Styron, sitting on her back porch overlooking a rolling lawn that sweeps down to the sparkling water of Vineyard Haven Harbor. "It is the most appealing place to sit still and write that I have ever known."

Rose writes and reflects from this spot, where she recently completed her aptly titled memoir *Beyond the Harbor*, which was written during the long COVID-19 lockdown. Two of her other books, *From Summer to Summer* and *By Vineyard Light*, are equally evocative of the Vineyard, filled with imagery of the island's "antique landscape" and "sweet fields."

Rose and her late husband, novelist William Styron, who penned books including *Sophie's Choice*, ran into playwright Lillian Hellman on their first visit to the island in 1958 and were quickly seduced by its beauty as much as by the literary community that has always been present. "It's a community of literature and art and politics," she says. "We all keep in touch and see each other a lot."

The Styrons bought their sprawling white summer home in 1965 with borrowed money, and Rose moved there full-time in 2013, several years after her husband died. Two outbuildings dot the property—one, a guesthouse where her four children and flock of grandchildren stay; the other, Bill's former writing cottage, with a "verboten" sign warning against interrupters still attached to its front door.

Rose no longer drops into her regular tennis game, but she still swims daily off her dock. An ever-widening circle of friends of all ages keeps her active, as do weekly Scrabble games, which Rose usually wins, and her energetic involvement in numerous local issues.

At home, she's a born entertainer and often hosts powerful politicians, award-winning filmmakers, fellow authors, and any extra guests at a moment's notice. To her delight, the Styron gene for creativity has been passed down and multiplied in her children and grandchildren, who are dancers, directors, musicians, and writers.

But above all, it's the island that continually sparks Rose's creativity, and in return, she does the same for the island. In 2020, the Martha's Vineyard Museum built the Rose Styron Garden, which was designed by another island artist, the world-renowned stone mason Lew French. The garden includes roses in honor of Rose and giant granite boulders where visitors can sit and read, write, or perhaps engage in a game of Scrabble. It's a fitting tribute to an island icon who, in her own words, says, "I am inspired wherever I am if I have good friends and a good view."

Rose's beloved Scrabble board becomes a writing surface when inspiration strikes.

BOSTON BOOK FESTIVAL

COVID Christmas 2020
greetings from mar...

Three
Depressed
MEN

Rose's love of family and literature
fills every nook and cranny of the house.

Rose's house with views of Vineyard
Haven Harbor

KRISHANA COLLINS

flower farmer

When Krishana Collins was young, she would visit her grandfather's peanut farm in Florida. The year she turned six–during a terrible drought–she noticed how dry the soil was and grabbed the nearest watering can to try to replenish the land. She's been tending to soil ever since: first as a vegetable farmer, and then, twenty-some years ago, after the death of her mother, turning to flowers. "I wanted to believe in life again," she says. "And I thought the best thing for me to do was to plant a flower field and watch them grow."

The field soon grew into her future career path as an organic flower farmer, now based out of the historic eighteenth-century Tea Lane Farm on Middle Road in Chilmark. A hand-painted FLOWERS FOR SALE sign marks the dirt road driveway that leads to the thirteen-acre farm. Krishana "bought" the former dairy in 2012, beating out forty other applicants to win the seventy-five-year lease from the town. She paid one dollar for the land and twenty thousand for the buildings, including the original 1756 farmhouse, which she is still in the process of renovating–one of the conditions of her lease. Neighbors' sheep graze in a pasture, and Krishana works on oversized tables in a stone barn, the concrete floor littered with a confetti of orange, pink, and purple flower petals that appear as though they are right out of a Jackson Pollock painting.

Krishana stays busy—she sells her farmstand bouquets weekly at the West Tisbury farmer's market, provides arrangements for local architects and parties, and has become the go-to Vineyard florist for weddings. "I really like it when brides bring me their ideas, or dreams, or visions that I can then interpret and translate," she says, adding that if a bride comes to her a year ahead of time, she can design what she is growing to fulfill that vision.

For Krishana, no two arrangements are alike. Her intent is for them to feel less like formal bouquets and more like someone has casually scooped up an armful of flowers from a wildflower field, yarrow weeds and all. "I like the flowers to be who they are," she says. "I want them to look like they're still growing. I like to show every stage of development—different heights, different stages of openings, even the buds."

To grow the more than one hundred and twenty varieties of flowers, including thirty different kinds of cosmos alone, she has adopted regenerative farming: not tilling the land, using cover crops, and respecting the soil. The farming itself is all-consuming for Krishana and her four full-time helpers. "It's not just work, it's your life," she says. "I feel like I don't have a choice. I just love to grow things, so it doesn't feel like an option not to do it."

"I promised to renovate the farmhouse. I want it to stay as it is but also want it to be comfortable and livable."

"I think people enjoy seeing people working with flowers. The movement and the activity, watching it evolve, seeing us plant, watching them grow and seeing them flower."

"My favorite flower is whatever is looking the best at the time, and it changes a lot."

Krishana at the farmer's market

NETTIE KENT AND COLIN RUEL

jeweler / artist

Jewelry designer Nettie Kent and painter Colin Ruel baptized their children by dunking them in the cove by the US Coast Guard Station Menemsha, just as Nettie had been blessed in Lambert's Cove the day after she was born. "It was our way of saying, 'this ocean is part of you,'" says Nettie.

The married duo grew up on the Vineyard: Nettie, the daughter of painter Doug Kent and her mother, Leslie, in the woods of West Tisbury, without a telephone or electricity; Colin, a member of a fifth-generation Menemsha family, in a house his grandfather built. They both knew that they wanted to be artists from a young age and spent their twenties developing their crafts in New York City, but they felt compelled to move home when Razmus Ocean, their first son, was born.

Nettie's hand-sculpted, textured, and tactile sterling and brass jewelry is inspired by the rocks she finds or the undulating waves she sees on frequent beach walks with her boys. It is all made in a bare-bones shed on their Chilmark rental property that Colin refurnished for her.

On the other hand, Colin's oil paintings are more direct representations of up-island sites and people, but with one slight twist. Rather than painting today's reality, he paints how he remembers the Vineyard looking in his childhood, ultimately giving his work a dreamy, romantic feel. "I am documenting this old way of living and the culture of this place," he says, noting the portraits he has done of island characters from his grandfather's generation. "I paint how it feels, not how it looks."

CREEK HILL

Though the two cannot afford to own a home on island, moving as much as twice a year to a range of lodgings, even a yurt, they recently opened the Ruel Gallery in Menemsha, which occupies the former garage of Colin's great-grandfather. His grandparents later used the space as a tourist shop, selling his grandmother's famous beach plum jelly and his grandfather's drawings. Now, Colin's paintings dot the jewel-box space and Nettie's designs are on display at the counter. But it is not limited to their art. It's also a spot for musicians to drop by and play and kids to dance while harbor buoys clang in the distance.

LEFT "Some of these characters I paint were my heroes growing up," says Colin with a portrait of Everett Poole, a legendary Menemsha fisherman.

LEFT Nettie's jewelry in brass and silver. BELOW Colin's handmade oyster knives, carved from the wreckage of an 1854 schooner

Nettie, Razmus, and Wyld
searching for treasure on
Lucy Vincent Beach

The annual summer opening
at the Ruel Gallery

Painting by Colin Ruel,
Brookside Farm

"I paint Middle Road a lot. It
feels like I'm coming home when
I get up-island," says Colin.

MARK CHUNG AND ERIC COLES

proprieters of lennox & harvey

We like the idea of the old town general store where you can come in and get a broom, or a sweater, or shampoo, but they are all a really cool design," says Eric Coles, who, alongside his husband, Mark Chung, owns the buzzy Lennox & Harvey—a general store for the modern day, as Coles describes it.

Located on Main Street, Vineyard Haven, the store was named after their respective grandfathers. "They were both well-dressed, well-read, and well-traveled musicians, and the names sounded good together," says Mark. "It works because they both had lasting effects on us."

Eric and Mark are equally well dressed and well traveled, with a passion for music that is evident from the retro-style turntable always spinning in the background. In the summer, one of them is bound to be behind the counter—they don't have outside employees—and during the off-season, the two spend their time scouring the globe for the unique products that help define the Lennox & Harvey brand.

Before moving full-time to the Vineyard, the couple cut their teeth in the New York design world: with Mark at Herman Miller and Eric at Ralph Lauren. For them, envisioning their goal and then transforming a dated, 1980s space into a clean-lined, lifestyle-oriented store came naturally; Mark even designed the industrial chic light sockets and installed the corrugated metal ceilings that were repurposed from an old barn. Mark and Eric had already transformed their Oak Bluffs cottage: going from floral pink and green decor to a minimal, graphic style that aligned with the store's

aesthetic, so much that their mid-century furniture, accessories, and cutting-edge art works can be regularly swapped out between the two spots.

At the store, the vibe is as intentionally relaxed and welcoming as their home. Customers become friends, friends become customers, and Mark and Eric's warm smiles and huge hugs—not to mention the occasionally proffered Aperol spritz—make it difficult to leave. In the three plus years since they became island residents, Mark and Eric have become a vital and vibrant part of the community, joining local boards, such as the Island Grown Initiative, and collaborating with artisans to design items including ceramic platters, tote bags, and jeans that are exclusive to Lennox & Harvey. "We found our tribe of like-minded people," says Eric. Their grandfathers would have been proud.

"We like the idea of the old town general store that everyone from the community comes in, and you know everyone," says Eric. "And you can come in and get a broom, but it's a really cool design."

Eric and Mark bring a little
Brooklyn to their home in
Oak Bluffs.

"Another reason we loved coming here is because there are so many farms on the island. It was my fantasy: Now we go to these farms and pick things up and cook," says Mark, a trained chef.

MARGOT DATZ

painter, muralist

Margot Datz built her log cabin-like home, which she describes as "Snow White on LSD," in 1979, shortly after moving to the woodsy outskirts of Edgartown. She started filling it up with art and still hasn't stopped. The moment she opens the front door, visitors are greeted with inspirational words—*Ingenuity*, *Kindness*, and *Honesty*—that are painted on each step of her staircase and flowers she created out of mussel shells that decorate the front door frame. She bathes in a backyard bathtub she calls "her church," and sleeps outside on a daybed piled with patterned pillows and swathed in mosquito netting until the weather gets cold.

A successful sculptor in New Orleans, Margot married a local fisherman and moved to the island, bringing a bit of that city's "juicy funkiness," as she calls it, with her. She quickly fell in with the artistic community, then based at the former Art Workers' Guild operating out of the Nobnocket Garage in Tisbury. "The thing that was notable creatively here was that it seemed like there's more time, as opposed to living in an urban environment," she says. "When I moved here, there wasn't much to do, so I had these unbroken swaths of time and that's where the big ideas enter."

And so she started painting. One of Margot's first projects, which put her on the island's map, was the painted murals at the Hot Tin Roof, the legendary eighties hot spot opened by Carly Simon. The club's first iteration featured lush, jungle-like imagery inspired by the French post-Impressionist painter Henri Rousseau, but in the mid-nineties, Margot looked to the more graphic, muscular style of celebrated mid-century island painter Thomas Hart Benton to create depictions of island locals. "I felt that if they wanted this club to work, they had to invite and embrace the beauty of the working class," she says. "I wanted carpenters and fisherman mingling with the millionaires." During the project, she and Simon became such kindred spirits that she has painted murals at Simon's house and illustrated many of her children's books.

Now Margot's fantastical, colorful tableaus of happy summertime scenes—frolicking marine life, mermaids, and fishermen—adorn island walls from the Oak Bluffs Steamship Terminal to the hospital and both up-island libraries. "I get a kick out of providing art for everybody," she says of her public work. "I get to see a lot of people enjoy art when they might not have otherwise."

In the past forty years, Margot has watched the island artist community triple, and it now includes her daughter Scarlett, who lends a hand on her work, and students from the high school who apprentice on some of her local projects. A treasured circle of friends keeps her company. "There are remarkable women here," Margot says, "and that contributes to creativity. We all started here in the late seventies, with houses decorated with fish trap furniture, and we've all soldiered on. It's been a remarkable ride."

Margot at work at the Old
Whaling Church in Edgartown

The original panels from Margot's installation at the Hot Tin Roof nightclub

Margot's annual summer art opening at the historic Grange Hall in West Tisbury

GOGO FERGUSON AND DAVE SAYRE

jewelry designer / jack-of-all-trades

The approach to the home of jeweler Gogo Ferguson and jack-of-all-trades Dave Sayre can best be described as a sensory overload. There's the music: guitars (plenty of them) and singing voices that are as sweet as honey; there's the smell of oysters roasting; and, of course, the sound of popping and crackling embers from an open fire. Outside on the deck twinkling lights, festive banners, and hand-me-down furniture create an inviting atmosphere that feels more like Mexico than Chilmark.

Surrounded by woods and conservation trails, the sprawling shingled house was a bed-and-breakfast when Gogo and Dave bought it in 2018. They immediately recognized the potential to renovate the home to welcome friends and family from far and wide. "I like bringing all walks of life together, whether they connect or not," says Gogo. "They usually do here."

This fellowship is possible with touches added by Dave, such as the large outdoor fireplace that he made himself, hauling rocks and ultimately creating the perfect oven setting for their nightly roasts of oysters straight from Sweet Neck Farm. "I have always been an artist wannabe," he says. "Somebody once said that my artistry is in the houses I build."

The music present throughout the home comes from an ever-revolving circuit of talented houseguests and one resident, the Grammy-nominated musician John Forté. John lives with

his family next door in the guest cottage and works in the basement recording studio he created and rents.

The guest cottage was a primary reason that they bought the house. John and his wife, Lara, rented their former guesthouse, and Gogo and Dave wanted to continue to include them in their lives. "I loved their whole vibe, how we all live together," she says. "It's like a commune."

When there isn't a gathering on the patio, John brings the kids over for dinner or nightly Scrabble matches. "There's a synergy, a togetherness, a harmony, a camaraderie that comes with being in a band," says John. "That's what living here feels like to me."

This casualness of island life suits Gogo and Dave, who also live on Cumberland Island, located just off the coast of Georgia, in a home that has been in Gogo's family for eight generations. Growing up walking the beaches with her grandmother, Gogo learned to find the beauty in the more overlooked elements of nature. Inspired by her surroundings, she now designs pendants with silver bird skulls, gold rings shaped like the bones of a raccoon penis, and bracelets comprised of shark vertebrae. "I think people just walk by this stuff," she says, "but I am constantly looking at colors and textures and shapes and incorporating it into some kind of wearable art." Gogo also designs sculpture: Her latest piece, cast in bronze from dried seaweed, hangs in the permanent art collection of the Martha's Vineyard Hospital.

The home's decor is also inspired by a prior residence of Gogo and Dave's, a house in San Miguel Allende, Mexico. Animal skulls of varying sizes sit on the mantelpiece, and thick Moroccan rugs add dashes of color to the dark-wood furniture inside. "Dave and I are collectors of everything from fabrics to pottery," says Gogo. "This house was a great palette to create an amazing expression of everywhere we've traveled and display all our photographs. These are the stories and the parts of our lives that I want to surround myself with."

Gogo in her home studio. "I find seed pods or bones walking the beaches. I do a whole line of mussel shell jewelry. My studio is filled with dried seaweed and all the collections from around this island."

A typical night at Gogo and Dave's, filled with music and friends

Scrabble is a competitive sport when John Forté comes over to play.

Dave roasts oysters nightly in his hand-built fireplace.

JOHN AND LARA FORTÉ

singer, songwriter / activist, photographer

I felt welcomed by the people, but I didn't necessarily feel the warmth from the wilderness or nature," says musician and producer John Forté of visiting his friend fellow musician Ben Taylor on the Vineyard in the late 1990s. He remembers asking Ben's mother, singer Carly Simon, for a flashlight one night to help guide him on the short walk to the guesthouse where he was staying.

"Carly said, 'You're from Brownsville, Brooklyn, you hang out in Times Square at three a.m., and you're afraid of some nocturnal creatures?'" John recalls. "And I said, 'Yes I am.'"

Now John lives in a cottage deep in the woods and breaks cow manure into dirt for the blooming pot plants he grows. "All that would've been anathema to me as a city kid," he laughs.

The path to living on the Vineyard–inspired by his visits with Ben and Carly, whom he now calls Mama C–was long and winding. In the 1990s, John had a successful career as a hip-hop musician and producer, earning a Grammy Award nomination for his work with the Fugees. But in 2000 he was arrested for cocaine possession with the intent to distribute, and he spent eight years in jail before Carly and Ben helped to get his sentence commuted.

He met his wife, Lara, at an island restaurant, and they moved in together three days later. Lara had her own background on the Vineyard: She grew up visiting Pohogonot Farm, the 350-acre compound of her step-grandmother's family. "My connection to the island came when I met Lara and we decided to make our life

here," John says. "When our children were born, that's when the roots started to get deep. And of course that coincides with my farming and getting my hands dirty. It wasn't overnight. It's been this slow, beautiful, natural transition that feels so right now that I'm on the other side, but wouldn't without the lived experience of jail and growing up in Brownsville."

John was still making a range of music and art and strongly encouraged Lara to return to her love of photography, even lending her his own film cameras and equipment. She began to focus on portraiture, using John as her first subject.

During their first year together, the two were doing what John calls "the Vineyard shuffle," bouncing around in search of year-round housing. Lara was pregnant with their daughter Wren, now six, when they rented a guesthouse of Gogo Ferguson and Dave Sayre's, located off Lambert's Cove Road. Now the two families live side by side in a new setup in Chilmark with a large field connecting the two houses.

John recorded his latest album, *Vessels, Angels & Ancestors*, in the studio he built at Gogo and Dave's house. The kids are free to come and go, and Wren likes to drop in to lend her vocals to an album or just see what her father is up to. "I remember her asking, 'Dad, are you working on a track?' I like the idea that she knows that I am working on a sound, and she knows that everything she is hearing didn't just materialize overnight."

Lara refers to John's pot plants as "his other babies." Farming is humbling, he says, but he recognizes that it's a gift to grow the herb. "It's the original incense. People vibe differently to it, and it's my way of having my own hand in cultivating energy that feels better."

The plants—and their artistic careers—are blossoming.

"It's every parent's dream," says John. "I am knee-deep, bearing witness to these gifts."

"I spend a lot of my time in my garden," says John. "I look forward to seeing my plants, listening to them, playing them music, watching them grow."

Lara's love for portrait
photography began with her
children, Wren Zazie and Haile.

KATE TAYLOR

singer, songwriter, artist

Every summer, singer Kate Taylor used to set up camp in Aquinnah, on land given to her by her parents. "Camp" was a hand-stitched teepee with a fire pit in the center, and no electricity or running water. Soon there would be a husband, two daughters, a stepdaughter, and even an outhouse, all coming together to create a little piece of heaven near the Gay Head Lighthouse.

"When you're sleeping on the ground with a little fire besides you and the Cosmos above you, you are of the earth," she explains.

Her parents had been Aquinnah pioneers who had bought nearly thirty acres of land near the Gay Head Light in the early 1960s. Kate, who often breaks into song while telling a story, is the younger sister of Grammy Award-winning singer-songwriter James Taylor, and the only girl in a talented family where music was revered and encouraged. She recalls endless Vineyard summer days spent outside "toolin' around the pond" with her four brothers, working at the counter at the Galley in Menemsha, and going to movies and square dances at the Chilmark Community Center, where she sang at talent nights.

By the time she was a teenager, the music scene, or, as her brother Livingston would call it, "the great folk scare of the 1960s," was exploding on the national stage and on the Vineyard. "Everyone was listening to it," she says. "Folk songs were having a heyday, and the Vineyard was a great place to be." The Moon Cusser Café in Oak Bluffs hosted some of the greatest acts of the day, and was *the* place to hear live music. "It was a coffeehouse and teens could go," she says. "I was probably fourteen years old."

One night, she and her friends saw folk and blues musician Tom Rush perform "Shimmy Like Sister Kate" at the Chilmark Tavern—a song she took personally as the only sister in a family of brothers. Her first album, *Sister Kate*, released when she was just nineteen years old, was named in honor of Rush and led to critical acclaim and a national tour.

But when the tours were over and she needed to feel grounded, she returned to Aquinnah and the land. She and her family did the Vineyard shuffle, for thirty-some years moving back and forth from winter rentals to the teepee and later to their little summer cabin. Her touring life was put on the back burner so she could be with her children, and it was then that she taught herself to play guitar. When her husband, Charlie, became ill, gypsy life was no longer sustainable. Kate's brother James offered them the guesthouse on his property—a move she jumped at. "If you live in a teepee, that's the job," she says. "And it's a great job, but you have to want it." She continued her songwriting—always inspired by the Vineyard—including "King of the Pond," about William Vanderhoop, a Wampanoag elder who sang to himself as he dug clams from the Menemsha pond.

Kate found another creative outlet in the beads she made from the purple and white Quahog clamshells found on the shorelines. "It's a way to honor the traditions of wampum and the native people," she says, and her bolo-style necklaces and charm bracelets regularly win blue ribbons at the annual summer West Tisbury Agricultural Fair. Ten years ago, she taught herself to paint: color-rich, expressive landscapes that evoke painter Thomas Hart Benton. And like Benton, who lived in Chilmark for years, she depicts empty Vineyard roads, stone walls, and

views of the same pond that Benton lived on.

Now, twenty years later, her guitars, tour memorabilia, paintings, and jewelry live in a rented Menemsha saltbox. She has moved out of James's guesthouse and has the plans and permits in place to build her dream house on the same spot of land upon which she once set her teepee.

But music is always at the heart, no matter where on the island she resides. She released her sixth album, *Why Wait*, in 2021, fifty years after *Sister Kate* first hit the charts. "Every single song—even the love and political songs—still has the thread of the Vineyard," she says. "I can't get away from it, I guess. But I don't have a reason to, because there are so many more stories to tell."

ABOVE *Kate's painting of her mother's road and Stonewall Beach*

BELOW *A shell bracelet made with quarters Kate earned from behind the window at her first job, at the Galley in Menemsha, at age fourteen*

OPPOSITE *Kate's blue ribbon-winning shell jewelry made over the years*

Kate Taylor's Two Town Tour

Tuesday, July 14, 2015

Aquinnah Town Hall • Showtime 8:00 p.m.

Wednesday, July 15, 2015

West Tisbury Grange Hall • Showtime 8:00 p.m.

Special Guests include Isaac Taylor

Tickets $25 at Alley's General Store and ticketsmv.com

Kate's painting of her AirStream, now sitting on the Aquinnah land of her future home. "Everybody was drawn here because it was the place where we felt the most lighthearted—the opportunity to be in a place like this in the summertime. Everyone just felt the magic of the place, and that exists still."

THINGS I CARRY

INTRO

1 — 4 — 1

E   A
B   E
E   A
B   E

E   A
B   E
E   A

Though there were two hearts beating
In two separate chests
And two blood streams coursing
And two different breaths

Two sets of eyes
Open to the world
And two pairs of hands,
My fingers in yours curled.

There was one bed we slept in
One path we strode
One love we carried
As we lightened each other's load.

You took me to the shoreline
And showed me treasure there.
You met me on a fog-draped dune
And smelled the fragrance in my hair.

GT

Am
Somethin bout
Em
enjoying the
Am
smething bout ridi
the turn of th

Am
something bout the
D
were born to be
Am
Smething bout vibra
D
you and me

I guess I showed you sunlight
And gave voice to your songs.
We tended the fire together
And the children came along.

Two swans upon the pond
Two heron on the shore
Two souls folded together
Through the forevermore door.

Am   *fm*
smething about, its ne
~~and was there~~ smethin *Am*
... Why wait

I have your love with me
I bring your words along
I can tune in to your wisdom, baby

HEATHER GOFF AND BILL O'CALLAGHAN

island folk pottery

A storybook world comes to life in the woods behind Island Folk Pottery in Chilmark. Life-sized tree spirits—in the form of wolf minstrels, flying dragons, and horned satyrs—hide among the brush of its sculpture trail, a scavenger hunt of surprises for those who walk the quarter-mile perimeter.

The creators, potters Bill O'Callaghan and Heather Goff, seem right out of a storybook too. Heather, a soft-spoken art-school-trained painter and guitarist, was born into an artistic family. Bill, a mason and carpenter by trade, arrived from his hometown of Cork, Ireland, in 1986 after meeting a woman from the Vineyard at an Irish pub. He only intended to stay for six months. Both Bill and Heather lived on the island for years before meeting at an Oak Bluffs artist cooperative, falling in love, and beginning a life together filled with art and playfulness.

Today they live in a house that Heather built "as a space for creativity," located just up the hill from the trail on family land next to her siblings.

Bill and Heather now share her overflowing ceramics studio in the basement. A well-loved potter's wheel sits on the patio just outside, shaded by a large umbrella found at the West Tisbury Dumptique. In the 1990s, Heather had a thriving ceramic tile business; Bill is self-taught, discovering his love of clay at Chilmark Pottery, the studio run by Geoffrey Borr. "I loved the people up there—the other potters and the people coming through," he says with

a twinkle in his sparkly blue eyes. "It was like West Cork, sort of hippieish and wonderful." In exchange for doing masonry on Geoffrey's house, Bill could use the pottery wheel, and he soon began to show his imaginative works at the artisan fair, eventually earning his nickname The Mad Potter. In their studio, Heather has carefully drawn a line in chalk that divides the shelf into two sides—his and hers—which is completely ignored by Bill.

Bill told Heather that his dream was to live in a place where people could come and experience his sculptures. "I had this idea to create a trail," remembers Heather. "So we each made work, and it just grew from there." The blue ceramic butterflies and masks peering out from branches are Heather's handiwork, as are the poems that hang from the trees. Bill constructs his tree spirits from pieces of driftwood that he finds on his daily beach walks with his Irish wolfhound Osheen. He then adds ceramic features, which turns each one into a distinctive personality. "Just seeing people come out of the trail," Bill says, "their eyes are alive and they have just experienced something. I receive the energy from these people, and it's such a joy."

The trail is open to the public free of charge. "There's something really spiritual about this land," says Heather. "To make it a commercial transaction takes away from that. We want people to feel renewed and discover things and go in with an open mind." Their future dreams include bringing in dancers from the Yard, hosting music nights, and building a studio for Bill so Heather can finally erase the chalk line.

Bill conjuring up fantastical creatures in the studio he shares with Heather

Nothing is wasted in the studio: pottery shards that Heather will reimagine into her mosaics

Bill says the musicians on the
sculpture trail "come alive and play
when no one is around. Sometimes
late at night when the wind is
blowing just so, I can hear their
merry melodies on the breeze."

"The tree spirits with their hands spread out, I feel the energy from them," says Bill.

FLAVIA GAETA

dj flavya

Word of DJ FlavYa's music and ecstatic dance workshops has traveled quickly on the Vineyard in the two years she's been on-island. The thirty-three-year-old Brazilian American music producer, whose real name is Flavia Gaeta, mixes traditional Brazilian and Latin sounds with hip-hop beats. She brings her headphones and turntables with her everywhere—open dances at the Orange Peel Bakery in Aquinnah, First Friday concerts at the Cove in Oak Bluffs, and among the goats and chickens at the Native Earth Teaching Farm in Chilmark. The audiences are full, happy, and ready to dance to the electric grooves of her music within the safe, alcohol-free ecstatic spaces she creates.

After spending time in New York City and São Paulo, Flavia moved to Martha's Vineyard in the fall of 2020, attracted by the island's natural beauty and beaches. "I was forewarned that housing was challenging," she says, "but I thought, 'Let's just try it.'" The pandemic was still rampant, so there wasn't a lot of DJ'ing around, but it helped that her sister and a vibrant Brazilian community lived there.

Flavia quickly got a job as a family counselor, and by the spring of 2021, businesses were beginning to open up, so she started DJ'ing. "I created this unique DJ position that had never been here," she says with a wide grin.

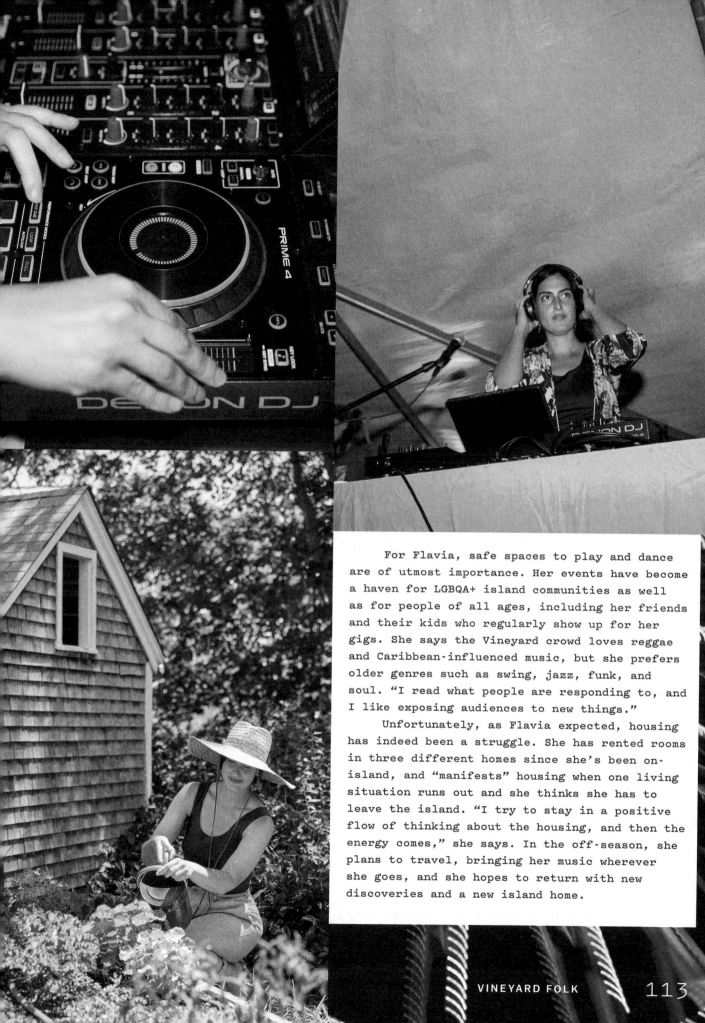

For Flavia, safe spaces to play and dance are of utmost importance. Her events have become a haven for LGBQA+ island communities as well as for people of all ages, including her friends and their kids who regularly show up for her gigs. She says the Vineyard crowd loves reggae and Caribbean-influenced music, but she prefers older genres such as swing, jazz, funk, and soul. "I read what people are responding to, and I like exposing audiences to new things."

Unfortunately, as Flavia expected, housing has indeed been a struggle. She has rented rooms in three different homes since she's been on-island, and "manifests" housing when one living situation runs out and she thinks she has to leave the island. "I try to stay in a positive flow of thinking about the housing, and then the energy comes," she says. In the off-season, she plans to travel, bringing her music wherever she goes, and she hopes to return with new discoveries and a new island home.

DJ FlavYa at work spinning tunes for the Vineyard crowd. "This is where I feel the most myself and most comfortable."

BEN TAYLOR

sports utility artist

I feel like I have always lived here," says singer/songwriter Ben Taylor. "It almost feels like I moved here ten years ago, but that's really just when I stopped leaving."

Ben and his sister, Sally, grew up at Hidden Star Hill, now their mother's property but originally owned by both parents: singers Carly Simon and James Taylor, who themselves each grew up coming to the island. Then, as now, he was surrounded by family: aunts, uncles, and cousins. And like his aunt the singer Kate Taylor, the Vineyard was where he came to "let all the steam out of my ears" after touring around the country with his band. Surrounded by his three rescue dogs while goats and miniature donkeys roam nearby, Ben explains how hard it is for him to leave the island nowadays: "I mean, I can do it, but it hurts. If you stay here long enough, it's like Velcro."

His beloved pets are just part of what keeps him on-island; Ben has also set up a creative wonderland on the lower section of the land. He travels the property—and the Vineyard—on a wheelie, a battery-operated flying skateboard that enables him to move at the high frequency his never-flagging energy requires. He says he finds a new trail every time he rides it off-property—from a beer run five miles away to a trip to the beach. "I have known the ancient ways around this island my whole life. I can go anywhere on this."

He lives in a small house, a short stroll from the barn that includes the professional music studio where he works. Though he has stopped touring officially, he is and will always be making and playing music—either solo or collaborating with other musicians. "Music has always been something that it's harder to tear myself away from than to make myself do," he says. "I always get motivated by other musicians who are around."

All of the covers and artwork for Ben's albums have been created on-island. But when he's not making music, he may be found operating a large Bobcat, digging up dirt, tree stumps, and rocks. A self-taught stonemason, he has built fire pits, outdoor kitchens, and walkways at friends' and clients' houses, including his own oversized fire pit worthy of a Burning Man installation. His pit came together naturally, he says, which is the way he prefers his rock assemblages to be. "None of the rocks have been changed in order to fit together," he explains. "You just have to keep turning them until they kiss—like people."

Outside his studio is a makeshift living room constructed from stone and locust wood that he calls "the Café." "It's like my green room," he laughs, describing how friends hang out there when a recording session is going on in the barn. "I am fascinated by the elements," he says, mentioning how he first studied Qigong and the Five Elements when he was sixteen. "And when you play with stone, you can make things that last forever."

An insatiable student of life, during the COVID-19 lockdown he took up Chinese, and he is in the process of writing some songs in Mandarin. "It's just one of those things like learning to play a new instrument. The notes are very different, but then you get your head around it," he says.

He has also become deeply engaged in a silk-screening project based on the Hot Tin Roof, the legendary Vineyard nightclub his mother opened in the early 1980s. Several years ago, he designed a rustic, hand-painted logo based on the original sign that he prints onto his extra never-worn T-shirts, recycled jean jackets, and sweatshirts. The T-shirts are a way of keeping the idea of the Hot Tin Roof—and the trademark—alive, and he muses on the idea of reopening the venue one day.

Perhaps he will be one of the first acts, performing one of his new songs. As he says in his gentle, poetic way: "There are so many songs out there ready to be written. I wait until a song is absolutely insisting on my involvement before I sit down and give it the time of day."

One of Ben's favorite toys, the Bobcat

Ben's hand-built "stone cafe," where musicians hang out on breaks while recording in the barn

Ben uses repurposed clothing for his Hot Tin Roof silkscreens.

ALLEN AND LYNNE WHITING

painter, partner / community collaborator

I'm a painter at heart," says Allen Whiting. "I farm because I was born on this piece of property. It's what I do and I love it, and it provides me with real inspiration at the oddest moments." He tends to forty sheep and a revolving coterie of pigs but says there's nothing that intrigues him more than the colors and light of a freshly cut field in June.

Over the past fifty years, Allen's oil paintings of beloved island vistas have become part of the Vineyard iconography and collected around the world. These soulful and richly colored landscapes, conveyed by Allen in loose brushstrokes, could only have been painted by someone who knows the island as intimately as he does.

When he's not setting up an easel on Quansoo Beach, Allen spends his days absorbing the life and rhythms of the family farm. His studio, the repurposed former schoolhouse of a nineteenth-century all-boys school moved from the town center, is crammed with canvases and coffee cans holding paintbrushes, along with artifacts he's found on his land. Animal skulls, doors, old bricks, and even a step from a nineteenth-century carriage once driven by his great-grandparents are on display, casually arranged in the wooden clapboards. "These things interest me," he says. "I am a romantic at heart, and they've been here for hundreds of years."

Allen's wife, Lynne, is a former schoolteacher who created the Education Department at the Martha's Vineyard Museum and

now heads the board of the Island Grown Initiative. They live next door in a large yet cozy farmhouse, circa 1850, that doubles as their gallery. When they had their first show in 1983, they painted the walls white to look like a New York City gallery and kept the space sparse because they didn't own any furniture. Several children and grandchildren later, the house is now full, vibrant, and welcoming, with the kitchen table at the heart of the home and paintings for sale on every wall. "It's a gift to be surrounded by Allen's artwork," says Lynne. "Having the public come into our living space has only enhanced our lives. Plus we get to educate them about the farm."

Vineyard artists have shaped Allen's work nearly as much as the surrounding ocean and farmlands. His grandfather Percy Cowen was an illustrator who taught the famous Realist painter Thomas Hart Benton during his time on island. Allen also grew up

admiring local role models and legends such as Wolf Kahn and Stan Murphy, who once lived in the farm's chicken coop, which Allen and Lynne also occupied before moving into the big house.

Allen now welcomes the next generation of young artists, his grandchildren perhaps even among them. "A lot of young painters are interested in what I do; you see a lot of them around. But I say, 'It's not my lighthouse, it's not my beach; you can paint it too.'" In fact, preserving the island's diverse creative community is foremost in Allen and Lynne's minds: They keep his painting prices steady and accessible, and they regularly donate works to island nonprofits. The Whitings have also bequeathed parcels of farmland to their children, helping to ensure that the family will be able to live and create here for years to come.

"I often wondered, when I was younger: Can a guy make an entire career within five miles of his home?" says Allen.

An empty easel
awaits Allen's brush.

JESSICA B. HARRIS

PhD, culinary historian

have always said I want to live where I can see seagulls," says Dr. Jessica B. Harris, culinary historian, journalist, and television personality enjoying a new round of fame from the Netflix series *High on the Hog*, based on her book of the same name.

On the Vineyard, she sees the birds easily from the front porch of her Oak Bluffs gingerbread cottage, just a five-minute walk from the ocean. Her parents purchased the cottage in the 1950s when Jessica was nine years old, on their first trip to the Vineyard, the house's advertisement from the New York Times in hand. "The 1950s were the 'glory days' for African Americans in Oak Bluffs," she says, with the authority of the historian she is. Now people have money, she says, but then, the summer community was made up of more middle-income homeowners: schoolteachers, administrators, and government workers like her own parents. She remembers camping out with her mother at the cottage all summer, racing down to the dock Friday nights to greet the last boat of the day, known as "the Daddy Boat" because it was filled with weekend commuters.

Sixty-odd years later, there are still some of the same families in the neighborhood. An only child, Jessica inherited the unheated cottage when her mother died in 2000. "The house is on Tuckernuck Avenue, and you tuck someone into bed, so it's named 'Harris's Tuck In,'" she explains, then emphasizing: "With one *n* not two." After nearly fifty years of college teaching, she has found herself spending more and more time there—"creeping further into the shoulder season"—working on projects like a food festival at the Martha's Vineyard Museum, a family history, and a new food history book. She may need to make room for yet another James

Beard Award; the ones she has now travel safely between her homes.

"Some portion of pretty much everything I have ever written has been done here," Jessica says of the Vineyard. These works include her acclaimed memoir, *My Soul Looks Back*, and *The Martha's Vineyard Table*, an exploration of the island's local cuisine and its culinary influences, as well as recipes and advice on finding the best pies and farm stands on island. Her first-floor office is crowded with books and paraphernalia, but she also works from a large, throne-like chair in the living room, known as "command central" because it faces the always-open front door and porch.

The porch is just one of many welcoming spots of the house. "I have a porch life that has ramped up significantly. People drive by and ask me if I'm the woman from *High on the Hog*," she says, laughing. She has been known to invite strangers in for a chat; recently Congresswoman Ayanna Pressley and Keisha Lance Bottoms, former mayor of Atlanta, stopped by. She also hosts an annual Bastille Day party, where she whips up bluefish spread and roast leg of lamb with local haricot verts from the farmers

market. "Food helps you fit in," she says. "Food means: You make your table, people come to it."

As a true New Yorker, Jessica doesn't drive, choosing to walk everywhere she needs to be in Oak Bluffs or hiring a taxi to take her to friends up-island or the West Tisbury Farmers Market. She's a regular there, usually accompanied by her homemade, extra peppery Bloody Marys in a Ball jar. "I have a route at the farmers market," she says. "Beetelbung for radishes, Grey Barn for bread, North Tabor farm for shishito peppers and sunflowers, the orchid lady, then flowers from Krishana, down to Morning Glory, and then the Vineyard Sea Salt." At the end of the season, she packs up what she calls "a truck's worth" of Vineyard bounty so she can take it back to New York.

All Vineyard food roads eventually lead to Jessica. She's often asked to moderate panels, host readings, and mentor other cookbook writers, which she does in her generous style. "I make space for others, I don't just stand on my spot," she says. "I am, and will die a teacher—I am just not in front of a blackboard."

"Martha's Vineyard is special. It's sanctuary and it's home."

"I find that I am engaged with the front door," says Jessica. "And it becomes a command center."

"Some portion of pretty much everything I have ever written has been done here."

AMY BRENNEMAN AND BRAD SILBERLING

producer, performer / writer, director

When I met Amy, my one thought was, 'Man, she better love the Vineyard or we are going to have a really hard time,'" says writer and director Brad Silberling about his now wife, five-time Emmy-nominated actress Amy Brenneman. He had fallen in love with the island after becoming obsessed with the film *Jaws* when he was eleven—the same film he also credits for sparking an interest in becoming a director. Luckily, Amy had her own history on the Vineyard, first vacationing there as a child and then teaching acting at the Yard performance space in Chilmark early in her career.

The couple bought their first house nearly twenty-five years ago and spend as much time on the island as their busy work schedules allow, lured both by the constant flow of inspiration and by the greater community. "When I come here, schedules fall away," says Brad, who has written several of his screenplays here, starting with *Moonlight Mile* in 2002. "I find that every part of my brain opens up."

At first, Amy's time on the island was used just to recharge from shooting her TV series *Judging Amy*—that is, until she took her first dance class at the Yard. "That's when the beauty and creativity started," she says. "During one class, they had the doors open, and it was a foggy day, and I got super porous with the nature and the creativity around me." In

2010, she went on to write her first play as an artist-in-residence there, and then turned an old garage on her property into a yoga and dance studio, with French doors that open to Tisbury Pond, to work out new pieces. "There I have the space," she says. "Literally and figuratively."

Their West Tisbury house is the hub for their two teenage kids and both sides of their family—Brad's parents had a house nearby until his father died in 2014. Hosting potluck suppers where friends play guitar and children toss beanbags on the lawn is their idea of a perfect kind of night. While Amy is musing in her studio, Brad says there are nine different spots on the property where he can sit and write for hours at a time, occasionally distracted by the resident Osprey family that he carefully monitors as they feed their hungry fledglings.

Sometimes, Brad escapes to write at a picnic table at the Menemsha Texaco Station, and he has even included a shot of the buoy there in all his movies—his own personal Easter egg to audiences.

But there's always time for their favorite rituals at home: kayaking or motorboating across the pond to the ocean, picking flowers and vegetables in the garden that Amy dreams of during the off-season, or sipping coffee under the trellis that looks out at the pond. "Right now there are so many types of service we are called to, and I don't feel tapped out when I am here," says Amy, who doesn't hesitate to lend her name, or her house, for various island causes. Yard dancers often borrow her studio for rehearsals, and the nonprofit Martha's Vineyard Shellfish Group works on an oyster restoration project from their dock, leaving piles of oyster shells.

"I am fine if I never leave this property," Amy says. "Each person has their center of the world, their axis mundi, and this is mine."

"We come here and breathe," says Brad. "It's the light, and we almost always have the breeze."

"I know I didn't make the zucchini, but I feel like I did. It's really thrilling to grow your own food. Everybody's jamming, everybody is growing. It's like we're all in flow."

Amy and Brad boat across the pond to get to the beach.

BOTTOM *The Osprey family who have made their home on the property. "They always come back, and they mate for life," Brad says. "We like to believe that somehow we made it hospitable for them."*

Oyster shells piled up near the pond.
Amy and Brad lend their dock to the
Martha's Vineyard Shellfish Group's
oyster restoration project.

The entrance to Amy's
beloved garden

MICHAEL JOHNSON

artist

I don't know how to describe the light here," says photographer Michael Johnson as he sits near the garden named after his father in his funky indoor/outdoor Vineyard Haven gallery. "It's a very specific light-sometimes it's gauzy, sometimes it's crisp. But the light here is stellar and great to work with."

The light is central to every photograph of the Vineyard he takes: luminous rainbows arching over Ocean Park in Oak Bluffs; panoramas of the bright-colored Aquinnah cliffs dappled with white snow; and the poetic images of African American swimmers on Inkwell Beach that made his name a decade ago.

Born in Harlem and raised in New Jersey, Michael first came to the Vineyard with a group of friends in the mid-1970s, camping out on land belonging to a friend's parents. He liked the island and regularly visited from New York, where he was pursuing music and visual art.

An April 1981 visit changed everything. He heard an R&B band play a couple of times, met a girl, and decided to move to the Vineyard and become a photographer. He moved by Memorial Day, took a day job as a house painter, rented a room for $200 a month, and later enrolled in a class in black-and-white photography at the high school. "I had no real focus then," he remembers. "The island was new to me, the camera was new to me; I was just shooting to learn the craft and create an aesthetic of my eye."

He quickly started taking photos, became absorbed in the local artistic community, and "learned how to live as an artist." He picked up juggling, started photographing the productions and actors of the Island Theater Workshop, and formed a band, Michael Johnson and the Miracle Cure, which later evolved into a gospel group.

The island was never far from his consciousness after he decided in the mid-1990s to move to San Francisco, where he could support himself selling his black-and-white hand-printed photography on the streets. He returned to the Vineyard often and even conjured it in his dreams: "I would be walking in this gauze-like light," he describes. "And then I would wake up and it was like a knife in my heart that I wasn't on the island."

He returned for good by 2008 and soon discovered what would become his best-selling print: the morning ritual of the Oak Bluffs polar bears, a group founded in 1946 as a safe space for African Americans to swim every morning at Inkwell Beach from July 4 through Labor Day. He titled the shot "Joy" for the moment the swimmers raise their arms from the water simultaneously, as graceful as synchronized swimmers, and chant: "I am the source of my joy and infinite possibilities."

That print now hangs as part of the permanent collection of the Martha's Vineyard Hospital and adorns hats, bags, and other merchandise he sells out of the gallery—all of which feels like a dream come true. "The shot is photogenic," he says. "But it is also very, very important, what they are doing here. Because the polar bears are central to the culture of Inkwell Beach, to Black culture, to Oak Bluffs culture, to island culture—all those things wrapped together in what they have been doing for decades and decades."

In the years since "Joy" was taken, he has continued to capture important, iconic images of the island and has become a critical force in the artistic community, including hosting a photography salon at Featherstone Art Center, where he brings in local photographers to share work and facilitate creativity. He keeps the gallery open from Memorial Day through Columbus Day, when he heads west. But he always returns to the island for several weeks in the winter. "It is a totally different place in winter," he says. "It is always good for an artist to have new inputs, just keeping some water in that well."

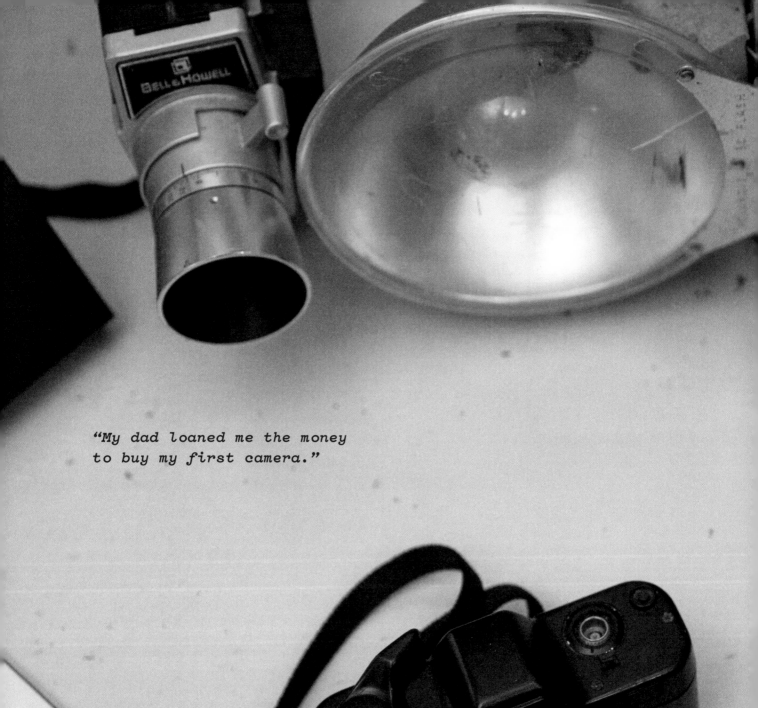

"My dad loaned me the money
to buy my first camera."

The Michael Johnson Photo Gallery, tucked down an alley off Main Street in Vineyard Haven

michael johnson photo gallery
- traditional/digital fine art photography -

welcom

"It just hits me. Not only is this photogenic, but this is very, very important, what they are doing here. Because they are central to the culture of Inkwell Beach, to Black culture, to Oak Bluffs culture, to island culture."

Joy by Michael Johnson

BROOKE ADAMS

actor, painter

In her 2016 mockumentary web series, *All Downhill from Here*, Brooke Adams fictionalized her life on the Vineyard as she and her sister, Lynne, bounded from island adventure to adventure, experiencing both real and made-up characters in increasingly hilarious setups. But the island—its beaches, trails, stores, and local landmarks—was always as big a star as the alter egos Brooke and Lynne played.

"It was really fun and we just came up with crazy things to do," says the celebrated stage and film actress, best known for her roles in the films *Days of Heaven*, *Invasion of the Body Snatchers*, and *Dead Zone*, as well as for starring in *The Heidi Chronicles* on Broadway. Brooke first visited the island when she was a young actress in her early twenties and fell in love with its natural beauty, the people, and eventually, the culture and theater. "I love the fact that you can come to this place that is so spectacularly beautiful and there's all this culture," she says. "We are just theater people; we can't go anywhere if there isn't a place to get involved in theater."

She and her husband, fellow actor Tony Shalhoub, of *Monk* and *The Marvelous Mrs. Maisel* fame, are involved in the Martha's Vineyard Playhouse and the Yard, performing in readings, plays, and benefits whenever called upon. The two bought a magical, rustic summer camp on a hill in Chilmark in the mid-1990s, which has since expanded into a sprawling, renovated main house, a guesthouse, and a barn for her daughter's horses. "It looks like a Western," she says, laughing, as Scoop, her wheaten terrier, Frito and Copper the

cats, and a sole guinea hen (from a flock that was originally twelve) freely roam the property. Her sister lives a short walk down the path, which makes for some lovely shared meals.

The walls of the house are covered with art by their friends—Edie Vonnegut, Kara Taylor, Heather Goff, Allen Whiting, and Kate Taylor—as well as Brooke's own work. She taught herself to watercolor while living in Spain in her early twenties, later taking classes as she was raising their two daughters. And now she paints colorful, impressionistic portraits in the open, windowed painting studio above the kitchen.

Though Brooke has also painted Vineyard landscapes, portraiture feels like more of a natural fit. "I was inspired by Stanley Murphy, honestly," she says, referring to the painter known as the Vermeer of the Vineyard. Like Murphy, Brooke captures intimate and representative moments of island characters both well known and not, such as Judy Belushi or Lee Vanderhoop, the postmaster of the Chilmark Post Office.

"I especially like to do people because I am trained in observing—that's what actors do. And portraiture is just like doing a character," she says.

Brooke is experimenting with new painting styles and hopes to start doing some writing again; most recently she participated in a Moth story hour at the Oak Bluffs Tabernacle. "It was terrifying and wonderful at the same time," she says. In the meantime, her 1984 drama film *Vengeance Is Mine* was only officially released in 2022 and opened to rave reviews. As a result, she's traveling the country to screen the film and take part in panels, first starting in her proverbial backyard at the Martha's Vineyard Film Festival. And to top it off, Harvard University has asked to do a retrospective of her work.

"I feel guilty that I am getting to do these fun things that don't feel like work," she says of her plethora of artistic pursuits. "It's just a pleasure; creativity is all I care about."

The house is full of flea market treasures and finds from the store Midnight Farm.

CAST OF
CHARACTERS

Brooke Adams - Open Studio

Father and Child and Scoop

Stop by August 11, 11am - 9pm
205 South Rd, Chilmark

works by
Brooke Adams

August 3 - 15, 2013

Opening reception August 3rd 6PM - 8PM

The
Vineyard
PLAYHOUSE
ART SPACE

24 Church Street, Vineyard Haven, MA
For more information visit brookeadamsart.com

Brooke Adams - Art sale

Stop by:

July 16

11 AM

to 5 PM

(Outside)

I CAN'T BREATHE

205

South Rd

Chilmark

All proceeds to benefit Black Ballot Power, blackballotpower.com
Supporting black community organizers and activists to get out the vote.

"I especially like to do
people because I am trained
in observing—that's what
actors do. And portraiture is
just like doing a character."

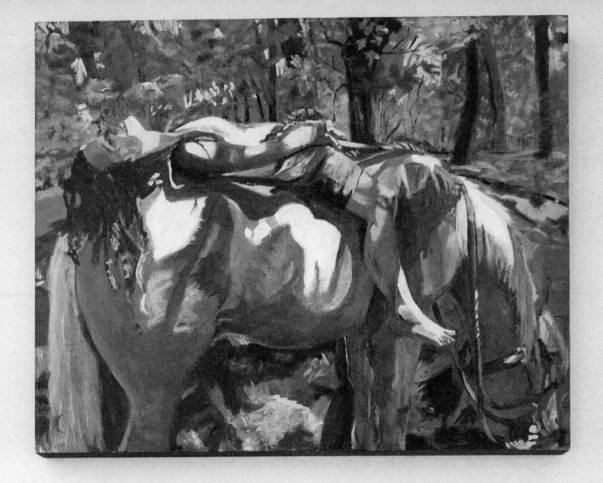

An old eel trap hangs from the
ceiling of the screened porch.
"I saw it as a work of art."

"There's something that really inspires you here," says Brooke of the island. "It's a mystery. Islands are very much a part of that, I think."

VALERIE FRANCIS

gallerist, curator

When Valerie Francis opened Knowhere Art Gallery with her husband, Ralph Grace, in 2019, people warned her that it might be tough exhibiting contemporary abstract and figurative art rather than traditional Vineyard landscapes. But in fact, the opposite has happened. Not only has business been great, but "people now come in and thank me for holding this space," she says with a warm smile.

Holding space—for art, yes, but also for ideas, conversations, and community—is central to Valerie's mission for her two galleries: Knowhere, located on Dukes County Avenue in the burgeoning Oak Bluffs Arts District, and Center of Knowhere, located closer to the Oak Bluffs action on Circuit Avenue, where Valerie and her family have been summering for three generations.

The galleries' names riff on her mission. "It's hard to have an understanding with one lens," she explains. "Ralph and I established this platform to be able to help influence and provide stories through the visual application of art. You have to *know where* you have been and *know where* you are going."

Knowhere's cozy, wide-planked, painted white space—a former nineteenth-century general store that catered to the gingerbread cottages of the Oak Bluffs Campground—has had a long history as an art space as the district developed: first as a potter's studio, then the Dragonfly Gallery, and, more recently, Josephine

Gallery. "The space has an energy around creativity," Valerie says as she points out a hanging of fabric collages by local artist Martha Mae Jones.

Center of Knowhere—a former yoga space—looks more contemporary, with a street front of paned windows and floating walls to display the work of artists such as Tracy Murrell, Stephanie Danforth, and Marion Wilson, who were all part of the exhibition *The Divine Feminine*. Valerie and Ralph live above the gallery in an open, loft-like space, and she often bikes between her two locations, a short ride around the corner from each other. Any downtime is spent rediscovering her childhood love of horseback riding, jumping, on her paddleboard, or spending time with her family.

Valerie first dipped her toe into the Martha's Vineyard art world by buying the building at 99 Dukes County Avenue, which now houses the nonprofit arts cooperative known as Galaxy Gallery. She soon started connecting and reconnecting with established Vineyard art world luminaries, including Ann Smith, a childhood friend and the director of Featherstone Center for the Arts, and neighboring Oak Bluff's gallerist Zeta Cousins, as she built her program of island and off-island artists.

In addition to exhibiting work that attracts her both on a visual and a storytelling level, Valerie has big plans for the galleries and the greater community, including hosting workshops and artist talks, as well as expanding the already popular art strolls of the district with food trucks and dancing. "I am just one of the notches in this long journey," she says in her soft-spoken voice. "So many people have come before me, and we are all here trying to generate artistic awareness and energy."

"First I see the image that attracts me, but then I want to know what their story is—who is the person? I am not a salesperson, so I need to have some other passion for being a steward. Everyone that I show, I love. They become almost family."

LEXIE ROTH AND EVA FABER

proprietors of goldie's rotisserie food truck

All are welcome at our table" is the motto of the Goldie's Rotisserie food truck, which is reinforced by the happy, vibrant sun and the rainbow-colored waves painted on it. The truck, run by Lexie Roth and Eva Faber, partners in life and business, pops up on weekends at the West Tisbury Farmers Market and Grange Hall, offering up rotisserie chickens, and seasonal sandwiches and salads, all with their slogan, "Handmade with love." "It's called Goldie's as an homage to the women in my life," Lexie says. "I did a painting series in the golden palette of all the women that I have lost. That is so important to me."

Lexie grew up summering in Aquinnah with her father, the well-known blues guitarist Arlen Roth, while Eva lived year-round in the woods of Edgartown. "I have the most beautiful childhood memories here—hopping on the Menemsha Bike Ferry to get ice cream, and no one is worrying about you because it feels like such a small town," says Lexie. Music also surrounded her childhood: When she was eighteen, she wrote and recorded an album in her father's recording studio at their house. "My creative heaven was the house and the woods and the ocean," she says. A working actress, Lexie still plays guitar and performs in the little downtime she has, still inspired by both her family background and the island.

"Every musician you would ever want to work with comes here and loves coming here." Despite their Vineyard backgrounds, the two first lived in New York and then quickly moved to the Vineyard full-time, like so many of their friends before them. After bouncing around various borrowed homes, they now live in a 250-square-foot unheated storage shed behind Merry Farm pottery. "Micah and Emily said, 'If you put the work in, it's yours,'" recalls Lexie. So, though there's an outhouse and an outside shower with a propane tank, they have creatively filled the cedar-paneled interior of the shed with soft kilim rugs, a sleeping loft, and a makeshift kitchen that still has enough room to hang the collection of knives they use cooking for Goldie's.

"It's like glamping," says Eva. "The best part is sitting on our beautiful porch. I wake up and am outside immediately." Of course, the rough Vineyard winters mean that they can only stay there from April through November before beginning the perennial search for off-season housing. "We are fighting to exist here every day just to run our business. We face wall after wall after wall. It takes a lot of patience and perseverance to trudge through," Lexie says. Still, they are determined to stay in this unique melting pot of an island where one can be both a professional musician and a professional chef. "We stay because it's home," says Lexie. "We want to make it work here."

"Word of mouth is
the only way to find
housing," Lexie
says. "We've lived
in a few different
places together."

wanna french?

...onion hot dog?

"Goldie's is our love child," says Eva. "The idea was to cater to people like us, island families on the go."

LOCAL VEGGIES ⋎ SALADS ⋎ COLD DRINKS ⋎ DESSERTS ⋎ SPECIALS

Goldie's
Rotisserie

~ VEGGIES
OF THE WEEK : ~

• FRESH MORNING GLORY
  SWEET CORN

• ROASTED SWEET
  POTATOES + CHICKPEAS

• BLACK BEANS

• NORTH TISBURY FARM
  MIXED GREENS

• PICKLED RADISHES +
  SPRING ONIONS

JULIE TAYMOR AND ELLIOT GOLDENTHAL

writer-director / composer

Every season has a different sound, depending on the animals. The bees are in the key of F or F sharp. You first hear the high-pitched insect sound around four forty-five a.m., followed by the birds."

Composer Elliot Goldenthal hears these sounds when he breaks from working on movie scores and symphonies all night in his bunker-like music studio. The studio is in the basement of the home he shares with his longtime love and collaborator, writer-director Julie Taymor, best known as the creator-director of *The Lion King* on Broadway, as well as several acclaimed films, including *Across the Universe* and *Frida*, for which Elliot won the Oscar for Best Original Score.

Elliot first saw the house back in the 1980s while on a beach walk with Julie's father. After spying the simple shingled Cape perched high on a bluff overlooking the ocean, her father remarked, "If I could live anywhere, I would live in *that* house." So it was serendipity when the house came on the market, nearly forty years later, and the couple bought it.

Serendipitous magic is a constant theme in their lives and work—and the island has played a large part in both. Julie just marked her seventieth summer on the Vineyard. As a teenager, she worked as a counselor at the Chilmark Community Center, and loved "hitchhiking, going up the dunes and rolling down, everything that's illegal now," she says, laughing. After she and Elliot met in their twenties, they would stay at her parents' house on Meeting House Road, where the two worked on the choreography and music for a production of

King Stag in the eighties, one of their first collaborations.

During the COVID-19 lockdown, they remained on island in their house on the bluff, with large windows facing the sea, enchanted by the natural world outside. "It was magnificent to see the animals come out and feel they could appear without being endangered by us," says Julie. "Just the snow on the Vineyard blew my mind, seeing the ice and all that foam that came up in Aquinnah, the water in the winter, all quality of life is just better here."

Her firsthand observations of the island's animal kingdom were inspirational to Julie while she wrote her latest screenplay, for *White Tiger*. "I would not have been able to write this in New York, I would be too distracted," she says. "Here, you just get up and go outside. It's a healthy balance for what writers go through." The creativity didn't stop there:

Elliot used the time to write a symphony for the Krakow Orchestra in Poland.

The two work on opposite schedules: Elliot through the night, while Julie wakes for an early-morning kayak or swim before settling down at the dining room table to work. They meet up in the late afternoons for daily walks across the dirt roads by neighboring fields dotted with sheep, as they ponder their next creative endeavor.

Together they bear witness to intense storms, mini tornadoes, rainbows, and sunsets that bathe the house with a golden light. "Just before the sun goes down there is such an incredibly bright contrast, like in a Vermeer painting," says Julie. "The light here actually has a tactile quality," adds Elliot. "When you go into the house, you can put the light into your pocket or save it and summon it later and it's there again."

"I work at night until dawn," says Elliot, in his basement studio. "I need to make a lot of noise without disturbing people."

"I am alone a great deal of the day, which is fine," says Julie. "And we get together in the afternoon and take walks and make dinner."

TIFFANY VANDERHOOP

jewelry designer

I t's important to represent indigenous designs, because they have been appropriated so widely," jeweler Tiffany Vanderhoop says of patterns such as Raven's Tail or the red-and-black zigzags on the earrings she named All My Ancestors. "By doing this, we are saying that we are the ones telling our story, we are the ones designing our clothes. We want to be the ones benefiting from our designs. It's important for people to recognize that."

Tiffany's childhood was spent shuttling between two different parts of the country and two different Native American tribes. Her father, David Vanderhoop, is Wampanoag, part of Aquinnah's vast and venerable Vanderhoop clan, and her mother, Evelyn, is Haida, who are from the Pacific Northwest. "I had such a deep connection to both of my cultures that it really stabilized me," she says. Tiffany's business was born from beads given to her from her aunt Diamond on her father's Wampanoag side. But her company's name, Huckleberry Woman, is the English translation of Tiffany's Haida name and refers to her long, curly mane of berry-colored hair.

Throughout her childhood, Tiffany was never away from Aquinnah for too long. Vineyard summers were spent climbing trees with her cousins, picking berries, and fishing for bass at Pilot's Landing on the North Shore. "It was always instilled in me that Aquinnah was my home. I felt a sense of belonging and interconnectedness with the land," she says while visiting the weathered farmhouse that is

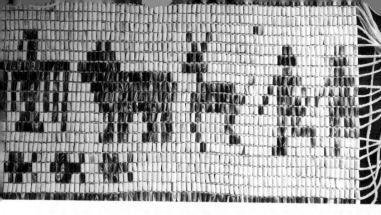

the Aquinnah Cultural Center, located near the Gay Head cliffs, the original nineteenth-century Vanderhoop homestead.

She moved to Aquinnah full-time in 2013 and started experimenting with jewelry, applying basic weaving techniques and beading earrings. She began to incorporate iconic images from the Wampanoag: purple triangles on her Aquinnah Wampum earrings to represent arrows, and the lyrical scrolls of the Double Curve design.

She also rekindled a relationship with a childhood sweetheart, Jason Widdis, a wampum jeweler. The two moved into the affordable Tribal Housing in town, and she started selling her work at a gift store on the cliffs. Her big break was getting accepted to the prestigious B.Yellowtail Collective, a cooperative and platform for indigenous designers. "That was a turning point," she says. "I couldn't even keep up with orders."

Now Tiffany is being recognized everywhere. Her earrings are eon an up-and-coming indigenous actress in the *New York Times*, on a soccer star on the red carpet of the ESPY Awards, on the cover of *InStyle* magazine, and in the pages of *Vogue*. Several examples of Tiffany's work are also in the permanent collection of the Museum of Art and Design in New York, and she is a regular at jewelry trade shows.

Tiffany and her family moved back to the mainland a year ago but return to Aquinnah as often as possible to ensure that her four children stay connected to their lineage and the land. As she walks through the rooms of the Aquinnah Cultural Center, musing on the rumors of Vanderhoop ghosts who haunt the place, she talks about an upcoming trip to the Santa Fe Indian Market. She will take a vial of red Aquinnah clay with her, as she does whenever she travels. But she leaves it when she comes back home to Aquinnah. "There's an energy here. You can feel it when you put your feet on the earth."

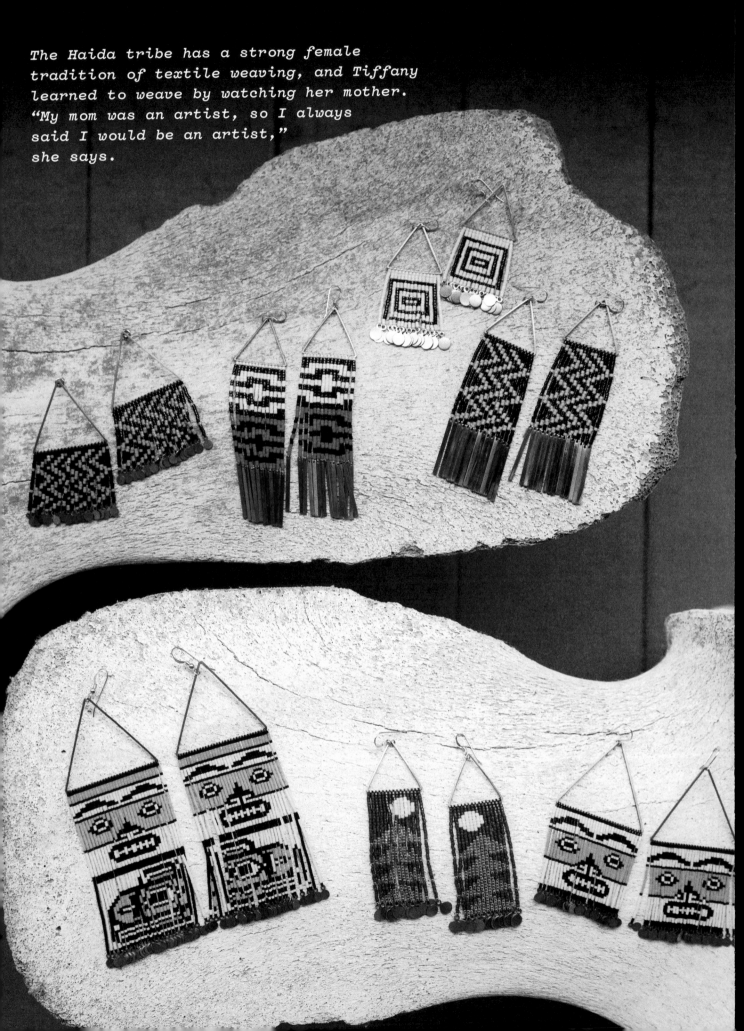

The Haida tribe has a strong female tradition of textile weaving, and Tiffany learned to weave by watching her mother. "My mom was an artist, so I always said I would be an artist," she says.

Aquinnah Wampanoag artifacts inside the Aqiunnah Cultural Center, the original Vanderhoop homestead from the 1800s.

KARA TAYLOR

artist

Kara Taylor is a self-described "Island girl" through and through. A painter and gallerist, she grew up in West Tisbury as a dreamy kid who drew daffodils in the spring and made drip sandcastles in the summer. She still likes to be close to nature, in both her life and her art. On her property, she dug the holes for the plantings herself and hand-built the stone walls that flank her gardens, and her work—images of moons, trees, and island waters—reflects that connection to the land.

Kara opened her first gallery twenty years ago in the former dairy barn of what was then the Nip 'n' Tuck Farm on State Road. There she grew and sold flowers and vegetables alongside her paintings of romantic Vineyard landscapes, which were often made moody with layers of encaustic wax. "My landscapes are usually where the ponds meet the ocean on the south side," she says. "They are not exact spots on the Vineyard. I borrow from what I grew up with, and I like to add some mystery."

After five successful years there and a seven-year stint on Main Street in Vineyard Haven, Kara relocated the gallery to its present site on South Road. She now rents the former gallery space of the legendary Stanley Murphy, the self-taught painter who chronicled Vineyard life for more than fifty years. He was also the spiritual godfather and inspiration to many island artists, so the space has especially good karma. People line up early to get into Kara's

annual summer openings just as they used to for Murphy's. "I have big shoes to fill," she says. "It's an honor to be selling art there."

Kara, like Murphy, sells her work at the gallery but paints at her home, located several miles away. Tucked away on a one-acre lot she procured through the island's affordable housing program—eligible only to local youth—she sketched out the house's gabled design, then relied on contractor friends to build the house from scratch while she painted the interior walls and sanded the floors herself. In true island style, she also bartered paintings for insulation and other building supplies.

The house itself, simple in structure but richly layered with her art and the work of artists she admires, was also furnished with the help of friends and family who gave her used doors, windowpanes, and hand-me-down furniture. "You can make it work with old stuff," she says, pointing out other vintage pieces found in salvage yards in and around New England.

A tireless traveler and explorer, Kara recently started spending the winter months in Capetown, South Africa, working at Sidestreet Studios, an artist co-op that she wishes also existed on Martha's Vineyard. The country has become her latest muse, inspiring mixed-media collages with evocative patterns and imagery. "I like new experiences. That's how I learn—by putting myself into [other] cultures," she says. "But when I come back from South Africa, I don't leave the house for a week. This will always be home."

Kara's home is full of salvaged pieces. The piano on the wall came over on a skiff from Naushon Island. "I hang this like a work of art, because the piano is my favorite instrument."

Kara's Marble Landscape in oil and encaustic on wood panel

Storm IV, oil, 23kt gold
leaf on wood panel

Kara's work space, just off her bedroom. She hopes one day to be able to build a freestanding studio on her property.

ZACH PINERIO

chappaquiddick wood company

Visiting Zach Pinerio and the Chappaquiddick Wood Company requires adding extra time to your travel plans. First, you need to get in the ferry line that snakes up from the water to North Water Street. Then, board the tiny three-car launch for the five-minute ride that transports you from bustling Edgartown to the small, bucolic island of Chappaquiddick, the island off the island. From there, it's a short drive on a country road that takes you past farm and flower stands to the turnoff for Whale Jaw Farm.

All of the company's woodworking, including salad bowls, serving boards, and other tableware, is done in the farm's barn, a beautiful, light-filled antique barn. The building stands at the crest of the hill on the historic property that Zach bought from the Land Trust in 2018. He works with local arborists and sources his wood from felled trees all over the island, naming the styles of bowls accordingly: Chilmark Cherry, Edgartown Maple, Circuit Avenue Pear. "To be able to make something from a tree from the island that people have a connection to is everything," he says.

The cutting board business sprung from Zach's desire to not waste any part of a tree: While the salad bowls are carved from the center of logs, the leftover parts can then be fashioned into smooth, oversized platters. Any marred or unusable wood is burned as firewood to heat his home; he can go through seven cords a winter.

One of only four practitioners in the United States who makes bowls directly from a solid block of wood, Zach taught himself to turn bowls through YouTube videos. And though he manages local properties to help pay the bills, the barn is his favorite spot and where he wants to spend his days. "When you are turning and when it works out right, it's really amazing," he says of his process. "You are quite literally dancing around the bowl."

Time out of his workshop is spent fishing at Wasque Point and slowly restoring the property's 1830 farmhouse, which still has its original floor planks and wainscoting. The farmhouse has become home for him and his wife, whom he first met on the island when he was fourteen. They met again twenty years later and recently married in the barn, among roaming chickens and under a mirrored disco ball.

The natural isolation of "Chappy," as locals refer to the island, doesn't bother Zach. He's been known not to leave the island, let alone his property, for months at a time. Living on Chappy is certainly a trade-off for convenience, but, as he says, "you wake up in paradise."

Zach bought Whale Jaw Farm in 2018. "It's the dream. I am just doing what I love to do—but for me: Can we just make this last another day, can we continue to do this? We will be the last generation, the artists who are here."

"Bowl turning is one of the only processes where you go from a log to a finished product."

Dancing is encouraged under the disco ball in Zach's barn.

We asked our Vineyard Folk where on-island

they go to tune in . . . or tune out . . .

EVA FABER:

"I take my dog to the state forest every day. It's my peaceful spot."

AMY BRENNEMAN:
"My barn. I work things out, because
I have the space literally and
figuratively."

BEN TAYLOR:
"A wise woman once said, 'Your chances
of kicking your opponent in the head
are very similar to your chances of
punching them in the feet' . . . Where
does that leave me?"

JULI VANDERHOOP:
"I love to go to my bees—there's
so much about a colony of bees that
humans are trying to figure out,
and if you really listen to them,
they help each other. They know
so much more than we do."

KATE TAYLOR:
"The place I feel the most at home is the northern edge of the cliffs, right below where my house is going to be, where the teepee was. That, to me, is the spot—it's close to home—it's ocean, shoreline."

BRAD SILBERLING:
"I wrote some of my favorite scenes bundled up at this table at the Menemsha Texaco station. It's an outpost and people come and say hello and get a cup of coffee or gas. It's so functional and banal, and I love writing there."

GOGO FERGUSON:
"My zen is walking beaches in the
fall on a rainy day collecting from
a new tide line."

NETTIE KENT:
"It's about the colors; when the rest of the island loses vibrancy in the winter. I can go to Lucy Vincent, and the blue of the sky against the red of the cliffs and the crash of the waves gives my eyes a fresh perspective."

MICHAEL JOHNSON:
"I love the Tashmoo spring: a beautiful, hidden-away spot; islanders don't ever go there. I go there at the height of summer—it's close and accessible and secluded, surrounded by the beauty of the island and just five minutes away."

JULIE TAYMOR:
"The walk down the path to the end of this point is my kind of heaven. On the edge of the world, eyes stretched over the ocean with constantly changing skies. The wind."

JOHN FORTÉ:
"My home, studio, garden. It's all
right here."

MICAH THANHAUSER:
"I like going to the
Brickyard and thinking
about the history and
the clay, and walking
the trails in the
woods."

MARGOT DATZ

"My bathtub is my church. It was
a fortieth-birthday present to
myself. I watch these trees grow;
they are so high, they tell me time
is moving on."

ERIC COLES

"I start on the beach in the sand, then spend half an hour swimming between the buoys. I start swimming in the ocean on May 21, and then I can stay in for longer and longer as it warms up. I stop swimming November 1, as sometimes there are snowstorms."

HEATHER GOFF:
"The woods here—and I really love
winter, the island winter. It's so
contemplative and you can sink in.
It's not necessarily a spot; it's
the rhythm of the island."

BILL O'CALLAGHAN:
"Lucy Vincent—it just has a grandeur
to it. You can see the clouds in
the distance, the grandeur, the
openness, the tide coming through—
there's always a sense of adventure
there."

ALLEN WHITING:
"On a very base level, caring for animals is head-clearing as well as being the foundation for the daily routine. Rain or shine, the animals must be tended to."

KARA TAYLOR:
"Where the Coca-Cola stream comes out on Lambert's Cove Beach. Whenever I am sad, I want to be next to the ocean to recharge my ions."

JESSICA HARRIS:
"I like to head up-island. Flip and Mitzi are good friends. I hang out there when the clangy gets a little too clangy down-island."

LARA FORTÉ:
"Being in nature and discovering new
places, spaces, views and vistas is
when I find myself."

BROOKE ADAMS:
"I like to go anywhere I can take Scoop."

ELLIOT GOLDENTHAL:
"The light in Squibnocket
has sound that inspires,
even in a darkened room."

KRISHANA COLLINS:
"Behind my house is a stream
that others say is a river. That
is the place I go so I remember
what nature, her very own self -
does on her own. It is perfectly
designed in every way from the
moss on the ground to the tunnel
of trees that leads you to the
bridge. And on the hottest of
days, I come from my open fields
to the dreamiest shade to cool
my feet in the ice cold water.
It is where I applaud all that
the natural world gives to us."

ROSE STYRON:
"Right here, looking out at my
view."

MARK CHUNG:
"There is a sense of calm and
clarity that I get while riding my
bike. Seeing the ocean and the pond
each day never gets old and always
makes me happy."

FLAVIA GAETA:
"Eastville Point Beach. It's deep
enough to swim, and you can see the
boats. There are no worries in my
mind when I am swimming; I love it
here."

ZACH PINERIO:
"My barn is my favorite place to
be. It's where I spend most of my
time and feel most inspired."

VALERIE FRANCIS:

"I love being near the water."

COLIN RUEL:
"My boat. I feel more connected with
nature, connected with my forebears.
I feel free and present."

LEXIE ROTH:
"Philbin Beach is where my soul
is, where I collected wampum when I
was little with my sister. It's so
special for me to go spend time in
the places where I spent time with
the loved ones that I have lost."

LYNNE WHITING:
"I fondly refer to this as 'The World.' It's my place of refuge, reflection, inspiration, and sweet welcome for newest family members."

DAVE SAYRE:
"Tiasquam Trail is the reason
we bought our house: its glow
of the moss and the sunshine
through the trees."

TIFFANY VANDERHOOP:
"Food gathering, picking berries, and preserving food gives me a connection to the land. When I was growing up, it was instilled in me that Aquinnah was my land, my ancestors' land."

OCEAN OF THANKS

Our first thanks go to Elizabeth Cecil, whose lovely manner put our subjects at ease, resulting in the beautiful and intimate photographs on these pages. She went above and beyond and was an invaluable partner and a joy to work with. We also want to thank our team at Abrams: Rebecca Kaplan, Juliet Dore, and Deb Wood, as well as our designers, Stephanie Huntwork and Darilyn Carnes, who helped realize our vision of creative lives on Martha's Vineyard so fully.

This book wouldn't exist without the talented artists who generously let us into their homes and studios to see where and how Martha's Vineyard has contributed to their creative expressions. Thank you. We hope *Vineyard Folk* does justice to the rich and full lives you have chosen and shared with us.

One of our aims for this book was to re-create (as closely as is possible in two dimensions) the feeling of being in the places and spaces of these artists; to that end, some chapters feature a background taken from a relevant element in the participants' lives: the denim from Juli Vanderhoop's apron, wood cross-sections for Zach Pinerio's story, an abstract painting from the walls of Valerie Francis's gallery.

An important subtext of this book—brought up in so many of our interviews—is the lack of affordable year-round housing on an island where the population swells from 15,000 to 200,000 in the summer. It is a problem that won't go away overnight and needs a lot of helping hands. We have just four hands, but with them, we are donating a portion of the profits of this book to the Island Housing Trust, a nonprofit on-island whose sole goal is to end housing uncertainty.

AMANDA would like to thank Tamara for bringing her into this special community and for being a partner so creative that she could've been featured in these pages. Giant thanks to the Bing-Ellis family, whose beautiful house has been my on-island base these past five years; Rachel Thebault and Stephanie Hunt for their recommendations and enthusiasm for this project. And last but not least, my two children, Teddy and Eloise Benchley, who have embraced this island as I have and who always provide me with love, laughs, support, and inspiration.

TAMARA would like to thank Amanda, co-author, collaborator, and friend; together we found our way into the heart of *Vineyard Folk*. I hope our dialogue around all things art and creativity will continue for years to come.

To my exceptional parents, Cora and Peter Weiss, who wisely settled in Aquinnah in the early 1960s, igniting my love for the Vineyard, and to my sons, Jules and Noah Stuber, for being the reason to move here, thank you. Judy and Danny Weiss, the best siblings to grow up with, always ready for an island adventure and ever willing to lend an ear, you are the most dependable, period. To Carly Simon, my lifelong friend and partner in numerous creative endeavors, thank you for BEING and for your extraordinary musical contributions to the world. To George Ahl, the greatest listener and hiking companion, endless gratitude for your unwavering friendship. Mitzi Pratt and Flip Scipio, thank you for saying yes at a moment's notice. Monina von Opel, Susanna Styron, and Kim Angell, thanks for your words of wisdom.

And to the hundreds of other creatives on Martha's Vineyard whose stories we have yet to share; we thank you too.